HOW?'D THEY DO THAT?

in...

ELIZABETHAN ENGLAND

Mitchell Lane

PUBLISHERS

P.O. Box 196

Hockessin, Delaware 19707

How?d They Do That? in...

Elizabethan England

Russell Roberts

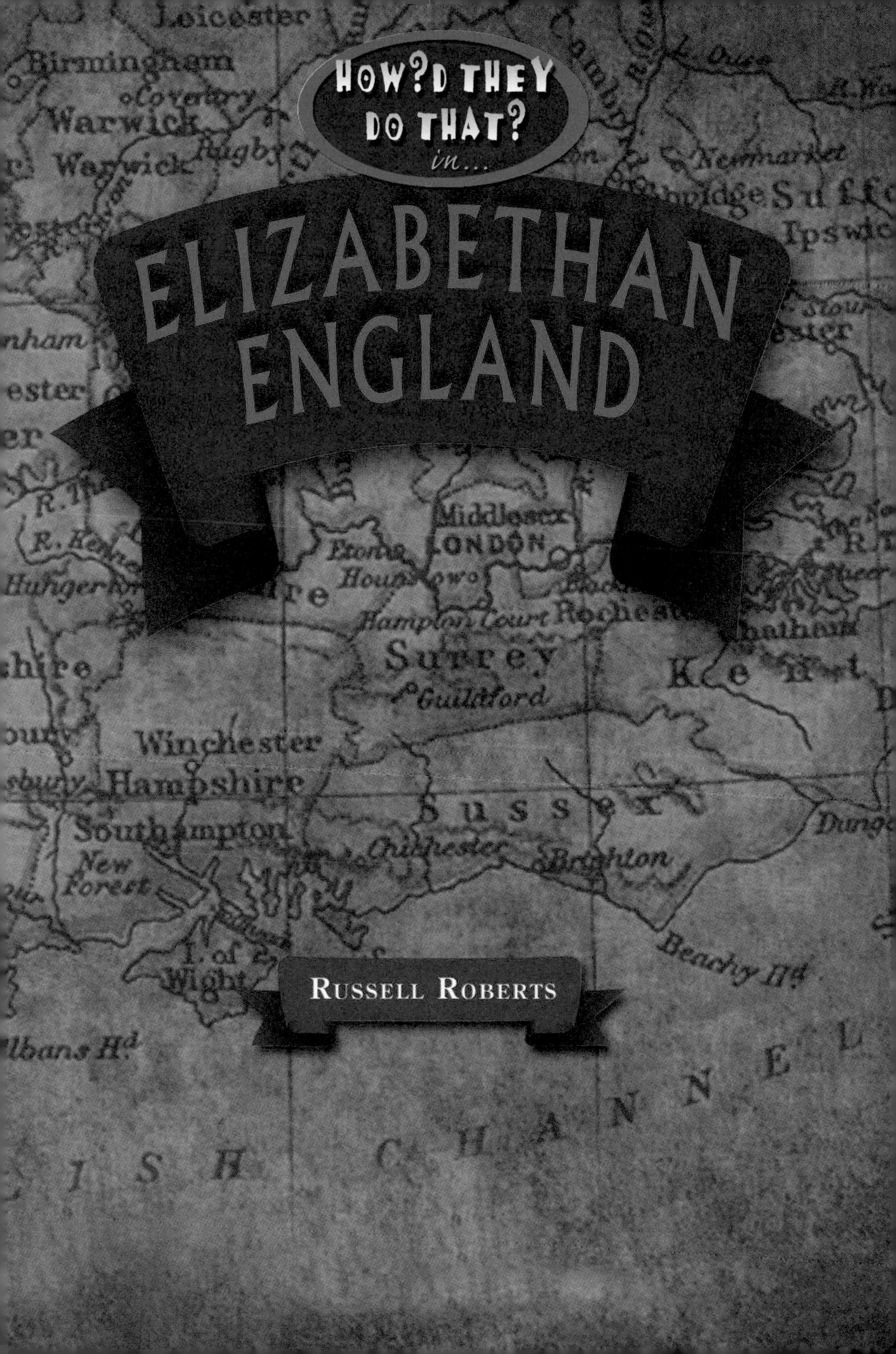

PUBLISHERS

J 942.055 Roberts

Printing   1   2   3   4   5   6   7   8   9

Library of Congress Cataloging-in-Publication Data
Roberts, Russell, 1953–
   How'd they do that in Elizabethan England / by Russell Roberts.
       p. cm.–(How'd they do that)
   Includes bibliographical references and index.
   ISBN 978-1-58415-823-3 (library bound)
   1. Great Britain—History—Elizabeth, 1558–1603—Juvenile literature. 2. Great
Britain—Social life and customs—16th century—Juvenile literature. 3. Great Britain—
Civilization—16th century—Juvenile literature. I. Title.
   DA355.R65 2009
   942.05'5–dc22

                                                                              200900130

PUBLISHER'S NOTE: This story is based on the author's extensive research, which he believes to be accurate. Documentation of his research is on page 60.
   Special thanks to Elizabethan scholar Cynthia Rasemas for her thoughtful insight in preparing this book.
   The internet sites referenced herein were active as of the publication date. Due to the fleeting nature of some web sites, we cannot guarantee they will all be active when you are reading this book.

                                                                                    PLB

CONTENTS

High atop a grassy hill in Cornwall in the south of England, an English peasant watched the action in the English Channel below. There had been rumors that Spain was sending its invasion fleet, and now the huge Spanish Armada, over 130 ships, had arrived. According to the sumptuary laws in existence at the time in England (commonly called the Statutes of Apparel), which dictated the type of clothing a person could wear, his clothing was made of wool. Around his waist he had a leather belt, not to hold his pants up but for hanging tools, knives, and pouches. On his feet he wore low-heeled leather shoes. Carrying a flaming torch, he rushed to the signal tower to ignite a fire that would warn everyone that the dreaded Armada had been sighted. As he touched the torch—a rag soaked in pitch and lit—to light the straw in the beacon, he wondered: How can poor England survive an attack and invasion by the most powerful nation in the world?

More than a century before the Spanish sent its famed fleet to overthrow England's Queen Elizabeth I in 1588, German astronomer

INVASION!

Regiomontanus had predicted that in the year of the invasion, there would be an eclipse of the sun and two eclipses of the moon. The planets Saturn, Jupiter, and Mars—omens of chaos and war—would be aligned with the moon in a menacing pattern. "If land and sea do not collapse in total ruin," Regiomontanus said, "yet will the whole world suffer upheavals, empires will dwindle, and from everywhere will be great lamentation."[1]

Conditions certainly seemed ripe for Spain to attack England. Ever since Elizabeth's father, King Henry VIII, had broken with the Roman Catholic Church in the 1530s, England had been in danger of invasion by the Catholic countries of Europe. They wished to return the country to Catholicism.

In 1570, the Pope declared that English Catholics did not have to be loyal to Queen Elizabeth, because she was (he said) a heretic. Following this line of thinking, while murder is normally a sin for Catholics, any Catholic who killed Elizabeth would be forgiven of the

King Philip of Spain had once tried to marry Elizabeth. After she turned him down, his hatred of her grew until finally he felt the time was right to invade England.

sin of murder, since she had been branded a heretic. No one knew how many English Catholics were unhappy with the new religion and might try to murder Elizabeth or rise up against her in rebellion. At the very least, England knew that there were powerful Catholic countries such as Spain and France that might invade in order to depose the queen and restore a Catholic ruler to the throne.

Spain and England had not always been enemies. When the unmarried Elizabeth had become England's queen in 1558, the Spanish king, Philip II, asked her to marry him. After stringing Philip along for a while, she finally refused him, and over the years relations between the two countries steadily soured. Spain had been behind several plots to oust Elizabeth. She in turn had not stopped English ships from raiding Spanish ones as they returned from Spain's New World Empire.

For more than twenty years, Philip had been urged to invade England and dethrone Elizabeth.[2] The invasion idea was called the Enterprise of England.[3] Then, in February 1587, came the final straw:

Mary, Queen of Scots, death mask

Elizabeth executed her cousin, Mary, Queen of Scots, who had been implicated in a plot to overthrow Elizabeth. Mary was Catholic, and many Catholics had always hoped she would someday become queen and return England to Catholicism. Now she was dead, and Catholics wanted vengeance.[4]

But for Philip there was another consideration. Mary had been half French, and if she had become queen of England, she would have been closely tied to France, Spain's rival. Now, with her dead, an attack on England would bring the country directly under Spain's—and Philip's—control.[5] It was time for the invasion.

In early 1587, Philip issued orders to begin assembling an invasion force for the Enterprise of England. In the spring of 1588, the Spanish Armada was ready.

And what a fleet it was! Spain had assembled 130 vessels in the harbor of the Spanish city of Lisbon.[6] The Spanish Armada contained everything from gigantic 1,000-ton galleons to little scouting boats. It took 8,000 sailors to man all the ships, which carried 20,000 soldiers for the invasion and conquest of England. In May 1588, the Armada left Lisbon Harbor bound for England.

Spain had made no attempt to disguise its preparations as the Armada was assembled, so England knew what was happening and had had many months to prepare. The country had used the time wisely, driving sharpened sticks into the beaches along the southern coast and building a network of signal towers

Spanish galleon

The Tudor rose graced the English flags.

to warn of the Armada's approach. As the bonfire atop each tower was lit, the person at the next tower down the coast would see it and light his. News of the Armada's approach burned across the English countryside.

The Spanish Armada was built at the height of Spain's power. To fight it, England had assembled a fleet of 47 well-armed ships, supplemented by a number of volunteer craft.

According to legend, when the signal fires heralded the arrival of the Armada, Sir Francis Drake, an English captain, was playing a game of bowls (lawn bowling). Drake casually finished his game before turning his attention to the invasion.

At first the Spanish managed to fight off attacks by the English ships and maintain their formation as the Armada moved up the chan-

nel. But on the night of August 7, the English sent eight ships ablaze with fire toward the Armada. That tactic scattered the fleet, breaking its formation. The next day, the English won a decisive victory at the Battle of Gravelines, off the coast of Flanders.

Tired, thirsty, and discouraged, the Spanish fled, setting a course for home around the British Isles and Ireland—they did not dare go back through the channel. More storms hit the fleet, and when it finally staggered home, it had lost approximately half its ships and two-thirds of its men.

Drake's exploits became legendary, and he is celebrated as the founder of British naval tradition. Spain tried to invade England several more times, with no success. Gradually Spain went into decline, and England became a world power. By standing up to mighty Spain, Elizabeth proved that England would not be pushed around, and its reputation grew among the nations of the world. England would use its navy to gradually establish itself as a world power.

The turning point in England's fight against the Spanish Armada came when the English sent fire ships to attack the Spanish ships. The tactic broke the formation of the Spanish fleet, helping to propel England to victory.

As a young woman, Elizabeth did not seem destined to become queen. She even spent time in prison! But she overcame the opposition to become a memorable monarch.

THE CULT OF THE QUEEN

Chapter 1

Few people have had an historical time period named after them. Queen Elizabeth I of England is one of those select few—her name lives on in *Elizabethan Age*. Not bad for someone who was disowned by her father, spent time in prison, and seemed unlikely to live to the end of her natural life.

Elizabeth I was a member of the Tudor family, which ruled England for nearly 120 years. The Tudor Age began on August 7, 1485, when Henry Tudor landed in England in command of an army of 2,000 soldiers. On August 22, Henry defeated King Richard III at the Battle of Bosworth, and Henry was crowned King Henry VII.

King Henry VIII, son of Henry VII and ruler of England from 1509, desperately wanted a male child so that he would have a son to whom he could leave his crown when he died. His first wife, Catherine of Aragon, gave him a daughter named Mary. He had his marriage to Catherine annulled and married Anne Boleyn, hoping that she would give him a son.

On September 7, 1533, Anne did indeed give birth to a baby: Elizabeth. Henry wasted little time getting rid of Anne. He accused her of cheating on him, and had her executed on May 19, 1536. Mary and her half sister Elizabeth were called illegitimate, and declared not eligible to succeed to the throne of England. Ultimately Henry had six wives.

Without a mother, and with a father who was not interested in her, Elizabeth's childhood was likely lonely. However, she had a good education, and was reportedly very intelligent.

Before he died on January 27, 1547, Henry VIII had a change of heart and put both Mary and Elizabeth back in the line of succession for England's throne. Upon his death Henry named his young son Edward (yes, one of his wives had finally given birth to a boy) to succeed him. The order of succession was Edward, Mary, and Elizabeth. But Edward, only nine years old when he became king, died in 1553, allowing Mary to become monarch. Mary was a Catholic who believed she had a divine duty to return England to Catholicism, and so England came under the Pope's authority again. She persecuted Protestants with such zeal she earned the nickname "Bloody Mary."[1] A plot against Mary convinced her that Elizabeth was involved. Mary imprisoned her

Mary Tudor— how different England's history would be if she had lived! Her early death opened the door for Elizabeth to ascend to the throne of England.

Henry VIII (center) and his six wives, from the top, clockwise: Anne of Cleaves, Catherine Howard, Anne Boleyn, Catherine of Aragon, Catherine Parr, Jane Seymour

half sister in the Tower of London for a time. But when Mary died of cancer at age forty-two on November 17, 1558, Elizabeth became Queen of England. The Elizabethan Age had begun.

Elizabeth, a Protestant, returned the country to Protestantism. She never married, and for that reason she was known as the "virgin queen." Many reasons have been offered as to why she never took a husband. One of the most common is that since her father had so many wives, she was against marriage. Elizabeth seemed to dislike the custom altogether. Many of the men whose company she enjoyed, such as Sir Walter Raleigh, ran into difficulty with Elizabeth after they married other women. Even the ladies who waited on her got into trouble with the queen if they dared to say they would like to marry.[2]

Many men were eager to marry the queen. King Philip of Spain, King Eric of Sweden, and Francis de Valois, the younger brother to the king of France, all wanted to marry Elizabeth.[3] Robert Dudley, Earl of Leicester, was probably Elizabeth's boyfriend. Elizabeth used her single status as a diplomatic weapon. As one of the most eligible women in Europe, all she had to do was imply that she'd like to marry someone, and his country would become England's friend. By the same token, she could easily scare another country by suggesting that she was considering marriage to someone, implying that those two countries would then be allied against each other.

The queen's court—those people with whom Elizabeth surrounded herself—was filled with love and laughter. It was a place of music and dancing, of plays, ceremonies, feasts, and games. During the Elizabethan

Elizabethan musical instruments were mainly stringed (lutes and harps); wind (flutes and recorders); and percussion (drums). People from all classes enjoyed church music, court music, theater music, and town music.

Today the English Parliament plays an important role in governing England. But in Elizabeth's day the Parliament was not as important, and could go for years at a time without being called.

Age, theater and play writing exploded in popularity. The great playwright William Shakespeare was a product of the Elizabethan Age.

But the court was more than just a source of entertainment. It was also the place where most of the important decisions of government were made. The queen would sit on her throne and listen to advisers, ministers, and others as they sought to gain favor or to influence Elizabeth in her decisions. The decision might be something as minor as settling a dispute between two noblemen, or it could be something as far-reaching as deciding whether to go to war.

Elizabeth and her court served as the executive branch of England, the highest governmental authority in the land. There was also a Parliament, which was similar to the U.S. Congress. However,

Eleven-year-old Elizabeth embroidered this book for Catherine Parr, one of Henry VIII's wives.

Pomanders filled with sweet-smelling herbs were used to disguise disgusting smells from waste and unwashed bodies. Physicians also believed that freshening the air with a pomander would prevent diseases such as the plague.

Parliament had a very limited function. It acted only when an existing law needed to be added to or changed by statue, and or in certain tax matters.[4] But Elizabeth could also impose certain taxes, and make laws herself by a royal proclamation (as long as it did not repeal or change laws made by statute). If parliamentary action was not required, there was no reason for Parliament to meet, and it was possible for weeks, months, and even years to go by between meetings. Out of the 44 years that Elizabeth was queen, Parliament met for just 35 months.[5]

According to Sir John Hayward, a contemporary who wrote about her, Elizabeth was a slender woman with a pleasant personality. Fair-haired, Elizabeth had large eyes. She was also well educated and could speak French, Greek, Welsh, Spanish, Italian, and Latin.[6]

She also had a powerful—and sometimes easily offended—sense of smell. At one time there was a French ambassador to the court who smelled particularly bad. "Good God!" said Elizabeth. "What shall I do if this man stays here, for I smell him an hour after he is gone from me."[7]

Elizabeth was popular with her people. In October 1562, she caught smallpox and almost died. Ultimately she recovered, but the entire episode brought renewed pressure on Elizabeth to marry. It was thought that if she married, she would have a child to succeed her on the throne. As long as she was unmarried and childless, her death would throw England into chaos, because she wouldn't have an obvious successor. But again Elizabeth resisted marriage. "I would rather be a beggar and single than a queen and married,"[8] she said.

In the 1570s, as her popularity spread, Elizabeth's Ascension Day—the day she became queen, November 17—began to be celebrated as a major holiday all across England. People rang bells, lit bonfires, and feasted. Elizabeth's Ascension Day continued to be observed long after her death—a sign of her popularity.[9]

At the court, the highlight of the festivities was the Ascension Day tilts. The tilts were like gigantic parades with knights. Often the knights would be on horseback or on floats, as in modern parades. Each float

Knights joust, or tilt, before an English king and queen. The contests were held in a large field. Commoners sat in the field, and nobles sat in a pavilion.

or group of knights had a theme. For example, one group might be dressed all in the same color costume and have the theme of honesty. As the queen and crowd looked on, the knights would joust (or "tilt"). After the tilts, the queen and her court would retire for a great feast.

Elizabeth would sometimes invite a foreign diplomat to sit beside her at the tilts. This person would watch the proceedings with her as Elizabeth talked politics, mixing business with pleasure. One day, after sitting through all the festivities, Elizabeth remarked that if she had known there would be so much said about her, she would not have shown up![10]

As the queen got older, the matter of her successor became more urgent. In 1601, Elizabeth's principal secretary and chief minister Sir Robert Cecil began secret negotiations with James VI, the king of Scotland, to have James take over when Elizabeth died. James was the son of Mary, Queen of Scots, so he was Elizabeth's cousin—and Elizabeth's closest living relative. Cecil intended to provide for a peaceful successor to Elizabeth and also to keep his job as a top government minister when Elizabeth died.[11]

In February 1603, Elizabeth began to suffer from insomnia. She lost her appetite and became frail. She hardly slept for nearly three straight weeks, and refused to let her doctors attend to her. There is speculation that she was worn out, and welcomed death.[12] Eventually her fever spiked and her throat swelled, perhaps indicating pneumonia or bronchitis. On March 24, 1603, the sixty-nine-year-old queen died, ending the Tudor dynasty. A few hours after she died, James was named her successor. The Elizabethan Age was over.

Elizabeth's funeral

Elizabethan Marriages

King Henry VIII's break with the Roman Catholic Church put his country on a religious course that it still travels. However, despite this and all of his other accomplishments, Henry is best remembered for his six wives.

Henry's first wife was Catherine of Aragon. In 1516, she gave birth to Henry's daughter Mary. However, by 1526, Catherine had still not given him a son. By then Henry was in love with Anne Boleyn and wanted his marriage to Catherine annulled—a special circumstance that would have to be granted by the Pope. When this did not happen, Henry broke England away from the Catholic Church and set up the king—himself—in the Pope's place, as the supreme head of the Church of England. Henry could then marry Anne, which he did in 1533.

When Anne couldn't produce a male child for Henry either, he had her executed in 1536. Soon after, Henry married Jane Seymour. She gave birth to a son named Edward in 1537, but she died from childbirth complications.

Henry VIII and Anne Boleyn

Henry married three more times. A popular phrase for remembering the fate of his six wives is "divorced, beheaded, died, divorced, beheaded, survived" (although technically the divorces were annulments).

Henry's many marriages demonstrate that royalty could play by their own rules, even with something as sacred as marriage. Most people, however, were not that lucky, and were bound by the laws and customs of the day. When a couple decided to get married, their intention to do so was announced in the local church for three Sundays or holy days in a row. This was called Crying the Banns. It was done so that any preexisting marriage contract could be discovered, or any other objections to the wedding raised. Elizabethans did not send out wedding invitations. Everyone knew everyone else in the local area, so guests just showed up. Presents were not usually given.

The woman contributed a dowry to the marriage, which was cash, property, or something else of value. This was given to the husband, and was his to do with as he liked. (The same could be said of the woman. She became his property as well.)

Streets in Elizabethan England cities were
narrow compared to modern city streets.
Buildings were often constructed quickly
and with no regard for their purpose, so it
was not unusual to have stores and homes
right next to each other.

LONDON CALLING

Chapter 2

During Elizabethan times, England's population was between three and four million people.[1] The country was overwhelmingly rural, with little industry. London, England's capital, and its largest city, had a population of approximately half a million.[2]

In London, houses, businesses, and taverns all existed side by side. Today we have indoor plumbing and waste treatment plants. Back then, chamber pots were used instead of toilets. The chamber pots were emptied right into the street, creating a smelly, slimy mess. There was no drainage, so the waste material just sat there until removed by rain, hogs, or other means. Birds called kites scavenged the streets, eating what refuse they found and building nests with the trash.[3] If nothing removed the waste material, citizens were required to shovel it into a cart and carry it away. Those who had a sterquinarium—a dung heap—at their front door were fined.[4]

Because the city grew so rapidly, London was a crazy-quilt mixture of cobblestone streets and narrow lanes. Many of the buildings were quite sturdy. Others, however, because they were constructed quickly on any plot of ground available, were poorly built. The streets were often dark at night, because there was no organized system of street-

People in Elizabethan London used the Thames River as a means of transportation. Traffic on the streets and sidewalks could be very heavy.

lights, as there are today. All homeowners were required by law to put a lantern with a candle outside their residence, but the candles often blew out.

London was walled on three sides. On the fourth side was the broad Thames River, London's main commercial artery. During Elizabethan times there was just one bridge—London Bridge—over the wide river. This bridge did not open to allow ships to pass, and large ships had to avoid it. The bridge itself was lined on both sides with businesses and homes, so the actual pathway for people and horses to use to cross from side to side was narrow. Instead of trying to cross the bridge to get to and from the city, people often used Thames water taxis. The taxi drivers would call out "Westward Ho" or "Eastward Ho," depending on which side of the river they were crossing to.[5]

The city's walls were built of ragstone, a type of blue-gray limestone. The walls had six main gates that opened wide enough to let men on horseback and carriages through. They also had some smaller openings that were just big enough to let a person walk in or out. No one was

in charge of maintaining the wall, so parts of it were always in need of repair. If part of the wall collapsed, a private person—such as a rich merchant—paid to have it fixed.

Outside the walls were the suburbs. Today, suburbs implies nice houses and well-manicured lawns. But in Elizabethan times, a "suburb" was a shabby, run-down area. In the suburbs, the rules of the city did not apply. For example, people who lived in the suburbs could use thatch as a roof for their home; thatch was forbidden in London because it burned so easily. They could also slaughter animals—a practice that was not allowed in London because the blood and animal waste created a horrible mess.

William Shakespeare's wife, Anne Hathaway, lived in this fifteenth-century cottage in Stratford-upon-Avon before she married. The thatched roof of the house was typical of the time.

A woman buys produce at an Elizabethan market.

London was divided into 26 wards. Each was represented by an alderman, who served for life.[6] The Lord Mayor, London's top official, was chosen each year from among the aldermen.

Since it was such a large city, London had many shops. Elizabethan Englanders did not "go shopping." Rather, they "went to market" or "to the shops." The greatest collection of shops in the city was at The Royal Exchange, which was built by Sir Thomas Gresham and opened by Queen Elizabeth herself in 1571. The Royal Exchange was (and still is) like a shopping mall—people could buy food and dry goods there, including perfume, wigs, and clothing.

Some providers of goods and services were called the same thing as today. For example, a tailor provided suits of clothes, while a lawyer offered legal services—just like now. But an apothecary dispensed drugs, a barber/surgeon provided dentistry, and cloth came from a mercer. (Today those same services are provided by the pharmacist, dentist, and mercantile.)

Because London was so crowded, and sanitation was virtually nonexistent, it was a prime breeding ground for disease. In particular, the deadly bubonic plague—which produces swelling in the lymph glands—seemed to be always present. Authorities would close up a plague victim's house and paint a cross on the door to warn others not to enter. Officials received reports from different parts of the city as to how many plague victims there were, and when the numbers got to a certain point, an epidemic was declared.

Elizabethans did not know the disease was spread by the fleas on rats; they considered the plague a sign of God's unhappiness. To avoid catching the disease, they would apologize to God for any sins they had committed. Other preventative measures included eating onions roasted with molasses and pepper, carrying cakes of arsenic under the armpits, and wearing special charms. (In modern times, people take antibiotics to fight disease, and they take preventative measures—such as not living with rats—to avoid becoming sick at all.)

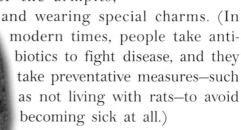

A plague doctor

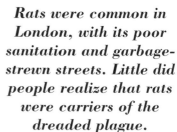

Rats were common in London, with its poor sanitation and garbage-strewn streets. Little did people realize that rats were carriers of the dreaded plague.

A plague cart approaches a victim's house to carry away the corpses. The plague killed people faster than they could be buried, so carters picked up the bodies and carried them to mass graves outside the city.

One of the dreaded jobs at the time was pushing the plague cart. Plague victims were brought from their homes and tossed into the cart. When it was full, workers would push it outside the town walls and bury the victims in a large pit.

London Trade Guilds

In order to work in any profession—from bookkeeper to bricklayer—a person had to join one of London's many trade guilds. There were three ways to become a member of a guild: If your father was a member, you automatically became one; you could become an apprentice to an existing member; or you could buy your membership.

The most common method was to become an apprentice. This was not a casual arrangement, but a very formal and legal one. Once you apprenticed to a master, you had to agree to stay with him for a specific number of years (usually seven). This was an excellent way to learn a trade. After the seven years were up, an apprentice became a journeyman, providing he proved to a group of guild members that he was able to adequately perform his craft. At that point he could work at his trade on his own. Eventually he would become a master and be able to take on his own apprentices.

A young apprentice

The master-apprentice relationship expected much from both parties. On the apprentice's part, the boy was to be a willing and eager student, ready to do whatever it took to assist his master and learn his trade. The workdays were long and hard—sometimes from dawn to dusk—and there was no pay; but holidays and Sundays were off.

An apprentice's life was defined by regulation. He was not allowed to wear fancy embroidered shirts or carry a sword—those were only for gentlemen—but he could have a club. He could not play tennis, but he could go bowling.

On the other hand, masters were expected not only to teach the apprentice how to perform a trade, but also to provide a family atmosphere that promoted good morals. The master was expected to produce both a skilled worker and a good and pious citizen.

Besides crops, Elizabethan farmers also raised livestock such as sheep.

ELIZABETHAN HOME LIFE

Chapter 3

The society of Elizabethan England was dominated by the upper classes, even though they constituted just a small percentage of the population. Most of the rest of the people farmed for a living. The lord—or boss—of the manor owned the land, and the workers farmed it for him. In return, the farmer was granted permission to plant some of the land for his own use.[1] People who did not earn land on which to raise crops for themselves could use land called the common waste.[2] Those who worked at non-farming jobs, as well as widows, could raise a garden or let their cow feed on the common waste. Sometimes this area was the only place they could get food.

The farmworkers lived in a small village consisting of a single street with houses on both sides. The village also included a few shops, such as a bakery, as well as a church. The lord of the manor owned the houses and shops—and the church!

Typically, a farm was made up of three large fields totaling about eighteen acres.[3] Two of the fields would be used for growing crops, and a third would lie fallow. This field would be reenergized throughout the year, with sheep manure used as fertilizer so that the soil would gain nutrients and be ready to grow crops the next year. Modern

A wooden plow

farm-
ers still
practice this
and animal
fertilizer. type of crop rotation,
manure is still used for

The fields were divided into strips that were
separated by unplowed grassy paths.[4] These
paths, called balks, allowed people to walk through the fields without
stepping on the crops.

Villagers who owned an ox would often combine their animals to
make a plow team of eight. There were different types of plows Elizabethan farmers used, depending upon the type of ground to be plowed.
Plows were made of wood and almost always by the farmer himself.

"God spede ye Plough, and send us korne enow [enough]."
Both men and women plowed—and prayed for a good harvest.

Cereal crops such as wheat were important for the Elizabethan farmer. August 1 or 2 was Lammas Day, the festival of the first wheat harvest of the year.

Smaller, lighter plows worked best on sandy soil, while clay soil took a broader, heavier blade.

If the harvest was poor, everyone in the village suffered. The English dirt roads were suitable only for walking or traveling by horseback, so it was difficult if not impossible to transport food from one section of the country to another. Thus an area that suffered a bad harvest, maybe because of insects or poor weather, had a hard time finding food.

Elizabethan farmers typically grew "corn," which is what they called cereals such as wheat, rye, and barley. They did not grow maize, the type of corn familiar to Americans. Maize could not grow in England because the weather was too cool.[5]

Sometimes, instead of growing crops, the lord of the manor might decide to raise sheep on the land. Sheep were useful because they could be a source of both food and clothing (their wool could be spun into thread, then woven into cloth). In addition to meat, sheep were valued for their milk. Six ewes could provide as much milk as one cow.[6] Land that was turned over to raising sheep instead of growing

crops hurt the villagers, who depended on farming the land to get food for themselves and their families.

Towns were larger than villages. Usually they had a population of about one thousand people and contained five or six streets.[7] The king or queen could grant a town the privilege of having a market day. Local farmers could bring their products to market and sell them to the general public. Market days were spaced out so that towns near each other did not compete by holding their markets on the same days.

The King's Highway connected all the market towns. Its main function was to allow the king's army to move easily around the country. For village merchants, the highway helped them get to market.

The Tudor era signaled the end of internal fighting that had wracked England. Thus, in Elizabethan times, houses could be built for beauty and style, and not just strictly as someplace from which to fight an invader. Gardens replaced moats, glass windows replaced narrow slots used to shoot arrows through, and nobles began to think in terms of entertaining their neighbors, not fighting them.

The houses of common people were made of cob—a mixture of mud with straw, chalk, gravel, and whatever else would make the mixture harden. Unlike today, little wood was used. Fireplaces heated the house. An Elizabethan innovation in the houses of commoners was the chimney, which let fireplace smoke out. Before that, smoke seeped through openings in the roof.

Abandoned monasteries were often used as a type of home improvement store. From the monasteries, stone, timber, tile, and tin (or lead) for the roof were obtained.[8] As late as the middle of the sixteenth century, glass was still a luxury. Each piece of glass had to be hand blown, then cut to make it flat. These small pieces were connected

with lead to form a lattice, or crisscross pattern. In this way, windows were made. As glass replaced horn windows or wooden shutters, Elizabethan houses became brighter inside.

The houses of the well-to-do were usually two or three stories tall, built around at least one courtyard, which could be enclosed or not. In the house was a great hall, a large room in which feasting and entertaining took place. On other days, the family would eat in the Great Hall. Most of the male servants usually slept in the Great Hall on palettes, which were similar to cots. During the day, these palettes were taken up so that the room could be used for other purposes.

The family of the house sat at the High Table, which was the main dining table. The other members of the household (such as servants) sat at "trestle tables." These were similar to sawhorses with boards

Hatfield House, built in 1497, was Elizabeth's childhood home and favorite residence.

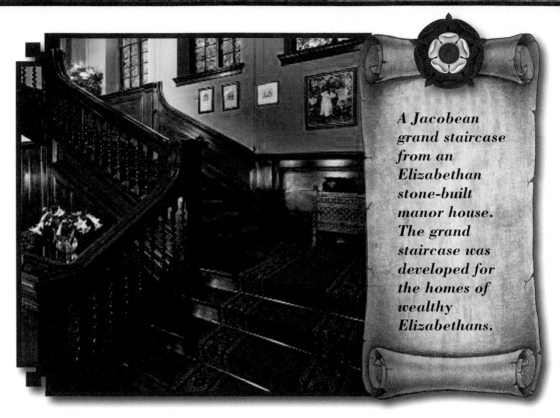

A Jacobean grand staircase from an Elizabethan stone-built manor house. The grand staircase was developed for the homes of wealthy Elizabethans.

placed on them.[9] Like the palettes, the trestle tables could be taken apart and put away.

One invention of the Tudor-era builders was the grand staircase.[10] Formerly, staircases had been small and cramped, and were built with battle and defense in mind. The grand staircase was a wide, sweeping passageway to the upper floors, often with beautiful wood carvings.

Upstairs there was a room called the long gallery. When they couldn't go outside, such as on rainy days, ladies gathered there to walk, talk, and perhaps do needlework. One curious thing about Tudor-era homes was that they did not contain a long corridor, or hall as it is called today. The rooms opened onto one another, so a person who wanted to go from one end of a floor to the other would have to walk through all the rooms, including bedrooms, to get there.

Chairs were a luxury item afforded only by the wealthy. Stools were used for sitting. Tapestries and other types of hangings were hung on the walls for decoration. As well as looking attractive, these had the added benefit of blocking drafts from cracks and seams in the walls.

Elizabethan Women

Life for women in Elizabethan England was not easy. Women were taught from birth that they were inferior to men—indeed, that they were the one imperfection created by God.[11] Poor girls were not given much, if any, formal education. Instead they were taught how to be good wives. They were instructed in tasks that would help them serve their husbands, such as cooking, running a household, and sewing. Upper-class women might receive a better education, but their role of serving their husband was still the most important.

In upper-class families, marriages were often arranged by the families for political reasons, such as to ally one family with another. Marrying for love was thought to be silly.[12] There was no legal age for marriage. Women usually got married around age fifteen, although they could be married even younger. Since upper-class marriages were arranged by the families, many couples did not even meet until their wedding day. Instead they had to rely on letters, portraits, and gossip to get to know one another. Brides did not traditionally wear white. Russet (a brownish pink) was popular. The idea of wearing a dress—like today's wedding dress—for one time only was nonexistent. The bride would wear a nice wool or cotton dress that would become part of her overall wardrobe. She would also wear a necklace, and flowers in her hair.

There was no such thing as a honeymoon for newlyweds. The bride and groom went to bed in the same house where the wedding feast—what today is called a reception—took place. A custom among villagers was for the bride to sell ale at the feast. This "bride's ale" sold for whatever amount each purchaser wanted to contribute to the newly married couple.[13]

A woman trapped in a bad marriage had no options. Divorce was virtually nonexistent. She could try to run away, but could expect little help or sympathy. She was considered her husband's property, like an ox or his house, and he could do with her as he wished.

Childbirth was very dangerous for women. Because there was little medical knowledge and no understanding of proper hygiene, many women died giving birth.

Westminster Abbey, where English kings and queens have been crowned since the coronation of William the Conqueror in 1066. Over a dozen monarchs are buried there as well.

OUT AND ABOUT

Chapter 4

Much like a person in modern society, the typical Elizabethan spent some time out of the home. People's main destination was church, for religion was always on their minds. "Religious talk was the talk of the day,"[1] researcher Mildred Campbell wrote in *The English Yeoman*. The religious battle between Catholics and Protestants gripped the entire country, and people rich and poor stood ready to argue the correctness of their beliefs.

In Elizabethan times, the Church of England, sometimes called the "new religion,"[2] was the official church. While being a Catholic was not a crime, there were no Catholic churches in England. It was illegal to be a Catholic priest in England, or to hold a Mass. Thus Catholics who wanted to practice their religion had a difficult time doing so. Everyone was required to attend church, or Prayer Service,[3] at least once per month.

For children, the main reason to leave home was to go to school. All schooling was voluntary, and most poor children did not attend. However, they received an education. Parents taught their children religion from the earliest ages so that they would be strong enough to resist the devil.

Children learned religion both at home and in church, and they were expected to pay strict attention. A person with a fuzzy understanding of religion could have his lack of knowledge used against him in court.[4] On the other hand, since most people were farmers, it was considered no big deal if a person was unable to read or write.[5] All they really had to know how to do was farm. If they needed someone to read or write something, the church vicar or town schoolmaster could do it for them.

Elizabethan peasants began to realize how reading and writing could help them in selling crops, drafting agreements over which and how much land to plow, and other matters. In their wills, fathers began requesting that their sons receive such education as was "proper to their degree and calling," meaning: only as much as they needed.[6]

Both girls and boys could attend grammar school.[7] In grammar school, reading and writing were treated differently. Reading was considered valuable because it was important to be able to read the Bible. Reading was also easier to teach, requiring nothing more than a book

Shakespeare's classroom at the Stratford school. Young William would have arrived at seven in the morning (six o'clock during the summer) and studied until five in the afternoon, learning literature in Latin.

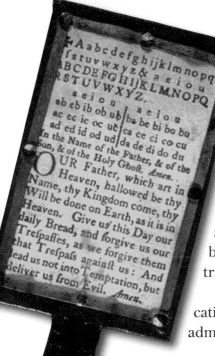

A hornbook

and a bench upon which to sit. On the other hand, writing required pencil, paper, and a desk or table at which to sit, and it was more time-consuming than reading.

In order to read, students used a hornbook to learn the alphabet. A hornbook was a wooden paddle with a short handle; it held a single sheet of paper on which was printed the alphabet, as well as some Bible verses. It was called a hornbook because the paper was protected by a thin, transparent piece of animal horn.[8]

If an upper-class man wanted a better education, he attended a university (only men were admitted to universities). After getting a degree, the man could become a teacher in that university, go into religion, or practice law. If none of those options appealed to him, he could just go home to his family's estate and live a leisurely life as an educated gentleman.

While traveling, upper-class Elizabethans could find food and lodging at inns. Taverns offered lodging and wine—but not food—again to upper classes. Peasants used alehouses, which could offer a combination of all three—food, drink, and lodging—and were the most common. An establishment that served mainly food was called an ordinary, so-called because it served standard food at a fixed price—not a restaurant as we know it today.

Another place that Elizabethans went, at least in the later years of the queen's reign, was the theater. This was the age of William Shakespeare, Christopher Marlowe, and other great playwrights. Theaters were helped by the popularity of a new occupation: the professional actor. Initially, members of craft guilds performed plays, but when they found they could earn enough money in this new field of acting, many abandoned their guilds to become paid, professional actors.[9]

This new class of actors had to be careful. Having quit their craft guilds, they were considered "masterless men" (people without jobs) and thus could be arrested and put in prison.[10] To avoid this fate, actors put themselves under the protection of the nobility. Technically, they were then employed as the nobles' servants, and thus had jobs.

Playwrights had to be careful not to anger the government. Before their plays could be performed, all plays had to be marked as "allowed" by the Master of Revels.[11]

At first, plays were performed outside, in the courtyards of inns. This was logical, since the inn was a center of social life as well as a gathering place for travelers, and so provided a captive audience. As late as 1575, there were no buildings in London that were specifically built as theaters.[12] However, going to the theater became so popular

A modern audience watches a play at a replica of the Globe Theatre, which officially opened in 1997. The Globe was built in 1599, burned down in 1613, and was rebuilt the following year. It was finally destroyed by the Puritans around 1644.

Elizabethans followed sumptuary laws, which dictated who could wear what colors, fabrics, and styles. Top, from left to right: middle-class dress; Tudor petticoat and dress (for the upper class); wedding brocade doublet, for upper-class men; lower-class woman's shift and man's shirt. Right: Whalebone corset, which upper-class women wore under their petticoats; red silk doublet, worn by upper-class men; and a lady's hat, to match the middle-class dress.

A falcon

that over the next thirty years, eight theaters were built. One of them was the Globe, completed in 1599. It became the main venue for Shakespeare's works.

Theaters were built outside London's city limits so that they would not be under London's rules and regulations. City officials took a dim view of theaters because they attracted large numbers of people who could spread plague or plot rebellions. Theaters were also considered fire hazards.

Another popular activity outside the home was hunting. However, what a person hunted was determined by whether he was rich or poor. The upper class hunted deer. Anybody could hunt fox, badger, otter, and squirrels—all considered "vermin."[13] In the same manner, while anybody could fish, upper-class gentlemen had personal fishing waters. Cockfighting was another sport for the upper class. Gentlemen paid great sums of money for a champion gamecock, or to have one trained to become a champion. Other popular sports for the upper class were bowling, archery, and falconry.

Bull-baiting and bear-baiting were popular throughout the classes. These were particularly brutal sports. A chained bull or bear was attacked by mastiffs, a breed of large dog, and had to defend itself from their deadly jaws. If a specific bear or bull became popular with the crowd, the people putting on the "show" would make certain that just enough dogs attacked to put the bear or bull in jeopardy, but not enough to kill it.[14] This way the favorite bear or bull could be brought back again and again, which ensured that large crowds would return. The bears and bulls were not the only victims in these sports. Many dogs also died in the fighting.

At the Theater

In Elizabethan times, there was no illumination after dark, so theatrical performances were held during daylight hours. Commoners attended only on holidays, because they were otherwise working. Typically, soldiers, law students, and upper-class women attended the performances.

Many people in the audience stood in the middle of the theater. Those who could afford it sat in galleries in the back of the room, while some of the more prominent (therefore wealthier) audience

Modern actors relive Elizabethan times, when men played every role—even those of women.

members sat directly on the edge of the stage. It is believed that the Globe, which is the theater most commonly associated with William Shakespeare, held 3,000 people. There was no air conditioning, no heat, and little ventilation. People sweated in the summer, froze in the winter, and smelled all the time.

Today actors and actresses in a play learn the lines for just one role, and they repeat the same part night after night as long as the play remains open. In Elizabethan times, actors could find themselves acting in five different plays on five different days. Furthermore, they might have two or three parts in each play. Thus, actors had to memorize all the lines for multiple plays, and be able to act in those parts at a moment's notice. Today a movie or play uses a lot of props both in the background and as part of the story. In Elizabethan times, props and scenery were almost never used. The stage was usually bare, so the audience had to imagine what the actors were describing and the items they mentioned.

Women were not allowed to be actors. Men played all the roles, both male and female. The costumes the actors wore were very bright and colorful. If they played multiple parts in a play, the actors must have spent a lot of time frantically switching costumes behind the scenes.

Elizabethans held festivals not only for religious reasons, but also for trade. Many towns had weekly markets, and larger towns had yearly fairs. Merchants from Italy, Spain, and other countries would come to trade, and jugglers and acrobats would entertain the revelers.

HoliDAys AND CuSToMs

Chapter 5

In Elizabethan England, people celebrated some holidays and traditions that are still observed in modern times. Others, however, have fallen into obscurity. Many of them are steeped in superstition.

The Christmas season was often called Christmastide.[1] It lasted from December 24 until January 6, which was known as Twelfth Day. The evening was called Twelfth Night, and was the last party night of the Christmas season. Gifts were not given on Christmas, but on New Year's Day. There was no Santa Claus–type figure like there is today. Common people gave gifts of oranges, rosemary, marzipan, and wine. The more well-to-do the person, the more elaborate the gifts they gave.

Sometimes the Christmas season was ushered in early, on December 21, by bell ringing. When this was the case, poor women could beg that day without fear of being arrested.[2] This was called a-goodling because it was considered good for a person's soul to give to a poor person.[3]

Another Christmas custom, also practiced at New Year's, was to make sure that a dark-haired man was the first to set foot in a house. (In some areas of England, it was a fair-haired man.) A custom that is still practiced is that of the Yule log. Men went into the forest, picked out a special tree, and brought a large piece of its trunk back into the house. They put it into the fireplace, and lit it with some bits of the previous year's Yule log. This was supposed to bring good luck—and protect the house from burning down—for the next year. Homes were decorated at Christmas with any type of plant that was still green at this cold time of the year, such as holly and ivy. This is still done today.

A game played at Christmastide was called flapdragon or snapdragon. People took turns picking raisins out of a dish filled with flaming brandy and putting them into their mouths. The object was to avoid getting burned.[4] Fortunately, this game is no longer played.

During Christmastide, the nobility was expected to put out a wide variety of food—one of the most popular dishes was called brawn, which was roast pork with mustard—and also furnish entertainment, such as dancers. The common people also feasted, and enjoyed dancing and card playing. Christmas is still celebrated with a special meal.

Good Friday and Easter were the two most important days on the Elizabethan calendar. Then, as now, both days were marked by church-

Suckling pig was, and is, a popular holiday dish. It is called "suckling" because it has only fed on its mother's milk.

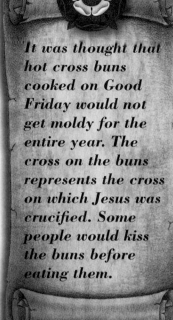

It was thought that hot cross buns cooked on Good Friday would not get moldy for the entire year. The cross on the buns represents the cross on which Jesus was crucified. Some people would kiss the buns before eating them.

going. Hot cross buns were a traditional food baked at this time, and they are still made today. But whereas they are just a sweet treat now, back then they were considered to be able to cure sickness in both humans and cattle. They were also considered good luck.[5]

Two weeks after Easter came Hocktide. During this time, taxes, tolls, and rents were paid—people got out of debt, or "hock." Other money would be raised as well; this was collected to repair the local church. Townspeople participated in sports, such as wrestling, and they also put on plays.

It was considered important to baptize, or christen, all infants as soon as possible after birth—an infant who died before being baptized would not go to heaven. In some coastal regions, people believed that birth took place as the tide came in, and death was more likely when the tide went out. (Some regions also believed that a man suffered birth pains just like a woman. In some cases, if the father of an illegitimate child could not be found, the village searched for a sick man, figuring that he must be the father.) Baptisms were a time for celebration. A child was given his or her name at the baptism, and a feast usually followed the ceremony. Presents of apostle spoons, each of which had an apostle carved on the handle, were given to the infant.

In Elizabethan England, people ate two large meals a day: dinner at around 11:00 or 12:00, and supper at about 6:00. However, people working in the fields might not eat until the light faded, which could be as late as 9:00. Schoolchildren, housewives, and working people usually awoke at 5:00 or 6:00 A.M. and ate a small meal called breakfast—so named because it broke their overnight fast. Foods at breakfast included beef, mustard, and eggs. Many houses in towns did not have kitchens. Food would be cooked over a hearth or taken to a cook shop, where it was prepared and picked up later. By the same token, many homes did not contain ovens. A person could mix ingredients for their bread, but then they had to take it to a baker and pay him to bake it for them.

A feast was an important part of the Elizabethan celebration of Twelfth Night. At the beginning of the night's festivities, a cake containing a bean was eaten. The person who found the bean would run the feast.

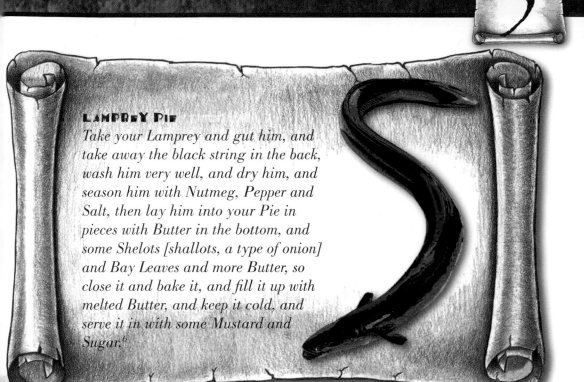

LAMPREY PIE

Take your Lamprey and gut him, and take away the black string in the back, wash him very well, and dry him, and season him with Nutmeg, Pepper and Salt, then lay him into your Pie in pieces with Butter in the bottom, and some Shelots [shallots, a type of onion] and Bay Leaves and more Butter, so close it and bake it, and fill it up with melted Butter, and keep it cold, and serve it in with some Mustard and Sugar.[6]

Elizabethan cooking was generally sweeter than modern fare. Meat was often cooked with fruit. Honey was used as a sweetener—unless you were wealthy. Sugar had to be imported and was very expensive. Since sugar was known to blacken teeth, it became a symbol of wealth to have black teeth. Other common flavorings were almond, cinnamon, and cloves. People were warned against eating raw vegetables—what we call salad—because it gave them gas. Indeed, some vegetables that are common today, such as the potato, were almost unknown in Elizabethan times. Instead, turnips and parsnips were usually used. Some people considered tomatoes to be poisonous.

Meat was a staple of the Elizabethan diet. However, meat could not be eaten on two days a week. One day was for religious reasons, but the second meatless day was to help the English fishing industry by making people eat more fish. If a person wanted to eat meat on a meatless day, he or she would have to buy a special license to do so. Typical meat dishes included beef, rabbit, deer, goat, and chicken. They were usually very salty, because salt was used to preserve them. Fish found on Elizabethan tables included cod, haddock, trout, and eels.

Bread was a part of every person's diet. Wheat bread was common for the wealthy, while those not quite as well-off used barley or rye to make bread. The poorest people made bread from beans, peas, oats, or acorns.

Elizabethans usually avoided drinking water because their water source was often a dumping ground for waste, garbage, and other refuse, and was full of germs and disease. Elizabethans drank perry (a slightly alcoholic pear cider), wine, beer, and ale. The wines were sweet and usually had to be strained before drinking. Ale was made from barley and flavored with a variety of ingredients, such as pepper, ivy, or rosemary. Ale made with honey was called mead and was enjoyed by all classes.

Elizabethans ate from trenchers, which were square pieces of wood with a round depression in the middle for food, and a small depression in the corner to hold salt. Forks were not commonly used. People ate with spoons, knives (usually their own), and their fingers. Napkins were not tucked in at the neck or placed in the lap like today, but slung over the shoulder or arm.

Like many things from the Elizabethan Age, although some things in their eating habits were very different than modern ways, other things were quite similar. Their time was a prosperous time for England.

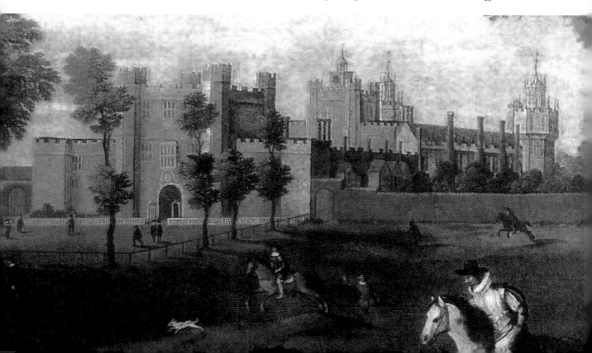

FYInfo

Superstitions in Elizabethan England

Superstition was very strong in the Elizabethan age. People commonly believe in ghosts and fairies. They thought that fairies lived in mounds of earth, and danced in fairy rings that they made in the fields. Unless bothered or mistreated, fairies usually left people alone. However, they were best avoided altogether. To keep them out of the house, people nailed an iron horseshoe to the door. (Today, people may nail a horseshoe to the wall for luck.)

Ghosts were a different matter. People believed that ghosts returned to the land of the living for a reason, and until that reason was found and the ghost was satisfied, it would continue to walk the earth. However, if the ghost was never satisfied, it would continue its existence unless someone could get rid of it. Sometimes a priest could exorcise (cast out) a ghost. Other times a ghost had to be driven into some type of container. Once trapped in there, the container was sealed so that the ghost couldn't escape. Once, for example, a black gamecock that was thought to contain a ghost was driven into an oven.[8]

People also believed in witches. There were two types. "White" witches, to whom people could turn for help—such as for locating lost objects, or for obtaining medicinal cures for sickness. Evil witches, who were in league with the devil, caused sickness and disease. They also controlled the winds— sometimes they would sell good winds to people

A witch feeds her familiars—animals that were thought to embody spirits.

heading out to sea—flew by broomstick at night, and could turn themselves into other shapes. It was considered bad luck for a pregnant woman to see a hare, because witches often turned themselves into hares.

Today images of witches on broomsticks have survived, but are mainly used in cartoons and for Halloween decorations.

Make Your Own Elizabethan Feather Fan

Fans in Elizabethan society were a symbol of status and prestige. They were also a required part of the upper-class wardrobe—for men and women. The feather fan appeared in the middle of the sixteenth century and rapidly became popular. Queen Elizabeth had over a dozen fans in her wardrobe, and she was often painted with one. You can make a feather fan using a wooden spoon or other inexpensive kitchen utensil and a few feathers.

Here is what you need

- Scissors
- Thick cardboard
- Duct tape
- A flat-headed kitchen utensil, such as a shallow serving spoon or spatula (available at dollar stores); if you can find one with a fancy wooden handle, all the better
- Glue
- Feathers (available at craft stores)
- Small piece of fabric
- Jewels, pearls, little mirrors, or lacy trim (available at craft stores)

Instructions

1   From the cardboard, cut the shape of the base of your fan's paddle. Make a

rounded piece, about 6" across, to cover the end of the kitchen utensil.

2 Duct tape the paddle base to the kitchen utensil, over the wide end of it. Fold the tape around the base, and use several layers to make sure it's securely attached to the handle.

3 If you want, use feathers of different colors to make a pattern. Use less expensive fluffy feathers as the base. Then, if you have them, glue fancier ostrich, peacock, or goose feathers on top. Using glue, cover the upper two-thirds of the base, front and back, with feathers, starting with the longest feathers at the top. Overlap the rows and fan them out.

4 Cover the base of the first row of feathers with a piece of fabric. The fabric can be rounded or pointed. Cut a hole in the middle for the handle. Slip the fabric over the handle, pull it up, and, when you like how it looks, glue it in place. Another way to cover the bottom of the feathers is to cut two pieces of fabric, then glue one piece to each side of the fan. You might also want to cover the rest of the handle with fabric.

5 Decorate the piece of fabric with jewels, pearls, little mirrors, or lace. Try gluing a piece of lace over the edges of the mirrors for a neater look.

TIMELINE

1485	Tudor Age in England begins when Henry VII defeats Richard III at Bosworth.
1517	Martin Luther nails his theses (a list of his grievances with the Catholic Church) to a church door, spawning the Reformation.
1533	King Henry VIII breaks with the Catholic Church.
1534	Henry VIII forms the Church of England (Anglican Church).
1547	Henry VIII dies on January 27. His nine-year-old son Edward VI becomes king.
1553	Edward VI dies. Henry VIII's daughter Mary is crowned; she becomes known as Bloody Mary.
1558	Mary dies, and her half sister Elizabeth becomes Queen of England and Ireland on November 17.
1559	King Philip II of Spain proposes marriage to Elizabeth. After a few months of courting, she refuses his proposal.
1560	Elizabeth refuses King Eric of Sweden's marriage proposal.
1562	Elizabeth nearly dies of smallpox.
1567	Elizabeth rejects the marriage proposal of Archduke Charles of Austria.
1570	Pope Pius V declares Elizabeth a heretic; therefore her subjects do not have to be loyal to her.
1572	Catherine de Medici of France proposes that Elizabeth marry her son Francis de Valois, who is a duke. The offer is refused.

1578 Catherine de Medici renews her proposal that Elizabeth marry Francis. Elizabeth refuses again.

1582 To correct errors in the calendar, the Gregorian calendar replaces the Julian calendar. Ten days are dropped, so the first day of the Gregorian calendar—Friday, October 15—follows the last day of the Julian calendar—Thursday, October 4.

1587 In February, Elizabeth executes Mary, Queen of Scots.

1588 Philip II sends the Spanish Armada to invade England and dethrone Elizabeth. The English defeat the Spanish at the Battle of Gravelines.

1589 Shakespeare writes his first play, *Henry VI, Part One*.

1595 The compound (using more than one lens) microscope is invented. It will be improved by Anthony van Leeuwenhoek nearly 80 years later to magnify over 200 times.

1599 The Globe Theatre, where many of Shakespeare's plays will be performed, opens just outside of London.

1603 Elizabeth I dies on March 24, ending the Elizabethan era.

1607 Colonists from England found Jamestown, Virginia.

1611 England's authorized version of the Bible, commissioned by King James I and called the King James Bible, is published.

1620 Puritans from England sail to America on the *Mayflower*.

Introduction: Invasion!

1. Bryce Walker, *The Armada* (Alexandria, Virginia: Time-Life Books, 1981), p. 63.
2. Ibid., p. 44
3. Ibid.
4. Ibid.
5. Ibid., p. 46.
6. Ibid., p. 67.

Chapter 1. The Cult of the Queen

1. D.M. Palliser, *The Age of Elizabeth: England Under the Later Tudors 1547-1603* (New York: Longman Group Limited, 1983), p. 15.
2. Jasper Ridley, *The Tudor Age* (Woodstock, New York: The Overlook Press, 1988), p. 49.
3. *Renaissance: The Elizabethan World; Life in Tudor England.* http://www. elizabethan.org
4. B. L. Joseph, *Shakespeare's Eden* (New York: Barnes & Noble, Inc., 1971), p. 115.
5. Ibid., p. 119.
6. Frank Kermode, *The Age of Shakespeare* (New York: The Modern Library, 2004), p. 22.
7. A.L. Rowse, *The Elizabethan Renaissance* (New York: Charles Scribner's Sons, 1971), p. 47.
8. Luminarium: *Anthology of English Literature, Queen Elizabeth I* (1533–1603) http://www.luminarium.org/ renlit/eliza.htm
9. Rowse, p. 34.
10. Ibid., p. 44.
11. Laura Marvel, *Elizabethan England* (San Diego: Greenhaven Press, Inc., 2002), p. 27.
12. *Renaissance: The Elizabethan World; Life in Tudor England.* http://www. elizabethan.org

Chapter 2. London Calling

1. Frank Kermode, *The Age of Shakespeare* (New York: The Modern Library, 2004), p. 43.
2. Ibid.
3. *Renaissance: The Elizabethan World; Life in Tudor England,* http://www. www.elizabethan.org
4. William S. Davis, *Life in Elizabethan Days* (Cheshire, Connecticut: Biblo & Tannen Publishers, 1994), p. 11.
5. Jo McMurtry, *Understanding Shakespeare's England* (Hamden, Connecticut: Archon Books, 1989), p. 96.
6. Ibid., p. 84.

Chapter 3. Elizabethan Home Life

1. Eric Kerridge, *The Farmers of Old England* (Totowa, New Jersey: Rowman and Littlefield, 1973), p. 40.
2. Jo McMurtry, *Understanding Shakespeare's England* (Hamden, Connecticut: Archon Books, 1989), p. 106.
3. Ibid.
4. Ibid., p. 104.
5. Ibid., p. 107.
6. Ibid., p. 110.
7. Ibid., p. 111.
8. *Renaissance: The Elizabethan World; Life in Tudor England.* http://www. www.elizabethan.org
9. Ibid.
10. McMurtry, p. 207.
11. Kelly Crispen, *The Tudors,* http://tudors.crispen.org
12. Ibid.
13. McMurtry, p. 121.

Chapter 4. Out and About

1. Mildred Campbell, *The English Yeoman* (New Haven, Connecticut: Yale University Press, 1942), p. 289.
2. *Renaissance: The Elizabethan World; Life in Tudor England,* http://www.elizabethan.org
3. Ibid.
4. Campbell, p. 262.
5. Ibid., p. 263.
6. Ibid., p. 265.
7. B. L. Joseph, *Shakespeare's Eden* (New York: Barnes & Noble, Inc., 1971), p. 109.
8. Jo McMurtry, *Understanding Shakespeare's England* (Hamden, Connecticut: Archon Books, 1989), p. 130.
9. Laura Marvel, *Elizabethan England* (San Diego: Greenhaven Press, Inc., 2002), p. 96.
10. Ibid., p. 97.
11. Frank Kermode, *The Age of Shakespeare* (New York: The Modern Library, 2004), p. 45.
12. Marvel, p. 99.
13. A. L. Rowse, *The Elizabethan Renaissance* (New York: Charles Scribner's Sons, 1971), p. 201.
14. McMurtry, p. 97.

Chapter 5. Holidays and Customs

1. *Renaissance: The Elizabethan World; Life in Tudor England,* http://www.elizabethan.org
2. A. L. Rowse, *The Elizabethan Renaissance* (New York: Charles Scribner's Sons, 1971), p. 232.
3. Ibid.
4. *Renaissance: The Elizabethan World; Life in Tudor England.* http://www.elizabethan.org
5. Rowse, p. 234.
6. Hannah Woolley, *The Queen-like Closet; OR, Rich Cabinet, Scored with all manner of Rare Receipts for Preserving, Candying and Cookery,* printed at the White Lion in Duck-Lane, near West-Smithfield, London, 1672; online at http://www.elizabethan-era.org.uk/lamprey-pie-old-recipe.htm

FURTHER READING

Books

Greenblatt, Miriam. *Elizabeth I and Tudor England.* New York: Benchmark Books, 2002.

Havelin, Kate. *Queen Elizabeth I.* Minneapolis: Lerner, 2002.

Lace, William. *Elizabeth I and Her Court.* San Diego: Lucent, 2003.

Marvel, Laura. *Elizabethan England.* San Diego: Greenhaven Press, Inc., 2002.

Stanley, Diane, and Peter Vennema. *Good Queen Bess: The Story of Elizabeth I of England.* New York: Harper Collins, 2001.

Weatherly, Myra, *Elizabeth I: Queen of Tudor England.* Minneapolis: Compass Point Books, 2006.

Works Consulted

Campbell, Mildred. *The English Yeoman.* New Haven, Connecticut: Yale University Press, 1942.

Chartres, John, and David Hey. *English Rural Society, 1500–1800.* Cambridge, England: Cambridge University Press, 1990.

Culbertson, Katherine E. *Elizabeth I: The Most Elusive Bride in History.* http://history.hanover.edu/hhr/94/hhr94_2.html

Davis, William S. *Life in Elizabethan Days.* Cheshire, Connecticut: Biblo & Tannen Publishers, 1994.

Guy, John. *Tudor England.* Oxford, England: Oxford University Press, 1988.

Joseph, B. L. *Shakespeare's Eden.* New York: Barnes & Noble, Inc., 1971.

Kermode, Frank. *The Age of Shakespeare.* New York: The Modern Library, 2004.

Kerridge, Eric. *The Farmers of Old England.* Totowa, New Jersey: Rowman and Littlefield, 1973.

McMurtry, Jo. *Understanding Shakespeare's England.* Hamden, Connecticut: Archon Books, 1989.

Palliser, D.M. *The Age of Elizabeth: England Under the Later Tudors 1547–1603.* New York: Longman Group Limited, 1983.

Ridley, Jasper. *The Tudor Age.* Woodstock, New York: The Overlook Press, 1988.

Rowse, A.L. *The Elizabethan Renaissance.* New York: Charles Scribner's Sons, 1971.

Walker, Bryce. *The Armada.* Alexandria, Virginia: Time-Life Books, 1981.

On the Internet

Briscoe, Alexandra. *Poverty in Elizabethan England.* BBC. http://www.bbc.co.uk/history/british/tudors/poverty_01.shtml

Britain Express: Elizabethan Life In England www.britainexpress.com/History/Elizabethan_life.htm

Elizabethan England www.culturalresources.com/Liz.html

Elizabethan England www.elizabethan-era.org.uk/elizabethan-england.htm

Life in Elizabethan England http://elizabethan.org/compendium/home.html

align (ah-LYN)—To join with others.

ally (al-LY)—To unite.

annul (an-NUL)—To abolish; to make void.

armada (ar-MAH-duh)—A fleet of warships.

artery (AR-tuh-ree)—A blood vessel that carries blood from the heart; a main transportation channel.

ascension (ah-SEN-shun)—A rising, such as to the position of monarch.

contemporary (kun-TEM-puh-rayr-ee)—Existing at the same time.

entity (EN-tih-tee)—Something that has a real existence.

herald (HAYR-uld)—A person or thing that comes before; also, a messenger.

hygiene (HY-jeen)—Bodily cleanliness.

illegitimate (il-ih-JIH-tih-mit)—Not legal.

insomnia (in-SOM-nee-ah)—The long-term inability to sleep.

joust (JOWST)—Combat between two armed knights on horseback.

lymph (LIMF)—A yellowish fluid containing white blood cells that is derived from the body's tissues.

Mass—A Catholic worship service.

monastery (MAH-nuh-stayr-ee)—A place where a group of people can live according to their religious vows.

phlegm (FLEM)—Thick mucus from the respiratory passages that is secreted through the mouth.

sumptuary (SUM-choo-ayr-ee)—Designed to curb excessive spending, especially on moral grounds.

superstition (soo-per-STIH-shun)—An irrational belief in the significance of a certain thing, place, or event.

supplement (SUP-lih-ment)—Something added to complete a thing.

Tudor (TOO-dur) **era**—Relating to the time that Henry Tudor and his family ruled England (1485–1603).

vengeance (VEN-jents)—Payback; revenge.

wily (WY-lee)—Crafty.

INDEX

ABOUT THE AUTHOR

Russell Roberts has written and published nearly 40 books for adults and children on a variety of subjects, including baseball, memory power, business, history, and travel. He has written numerous books for Mitchell Lane Publishers, including Nathaniel Hawthorne, Holidays and Celebrations in Colonial America, What's So Great About Daniel Boone, Poseidon, The Life and Times of Nostradamus, *and* The Lost Continent of Atlantis. *He lives in Bordentown, New Jersey, with his family and a fat, fuzzy, crafty calico cat named Rusti.*